GHOST OF A PERSON PASSING IN FRONT OF THE FLAG

Poems

D.F. Brown

BLOOMSDAY

Published in the United States by Bloomsday

bloomsdayliterary.com
Houston, Texas

ISBN 978-0-9998239-1-0

Library of Congress Control Number
2018934015

Printed in the United States of America

FIRST EDITION

The lines from Robert Creeley are quoted from *Pieces* (Scribner, 1969).

Cover artwork by Randy Twaddle

Interior photos by T.J. Amick, 1968–69,
Quang Ngai, Vietnam. 196th Light Infantry Brigade

Portrait photography by Paula Nguyen Luu

Book design by Houston Creative Space

for Tracye Wear

CONTENTS

Part One

GHOST
OF
A
PERSON
PASSING
IN
FRONT
OF
THE
FLAG

PART ONE

The "present dented,"
call it "long
distance," come
here home.

—Robert Creeley

GHOST OF A PERSON PASSING IN FRONT OF THE FLAG

When I was king in Vietnam
they loved us for the body count.

We choppered everywhere
searching for some peace with honor

FRACTURED FAIRY TALE

Once upon a time
from the left
your left
you're left right

at the start beginning
this is the fuck you part
between history and a hard place
many torn and bloodied boys
twisted into facts

them in fucking salad suits
as if the past were true
and grinning in a faded Polaroid

teenagers posing *johnwayned*
them in fucking salad suits
hand to hand in the syllables

and no bread crumbs

WHATEVER HAPPENS MERGES

The first day I didn't know
how far to anywhere
though the Sarge pointed out
sandbagged bunkers
left and right
laced in triple concertina wire,
enlisted outhouse, commo trench
and wiring to the claymores—
all I saw was leaky sandbags
in a blast wall around the ammo
and the sun's red knot at the horizon.
Then night fell just like it was supposed to
and the wind whispered its old story,
I listened close as words
to my soul squeak and squeal.

KEEPING DAYS AND NUMBERS TOGETHER

Now this is halfway round the world,
the other side with all its smell
and it's almost like

you don't have to care
or there is no need
until somebody *eats it*,

buys the farm and then
all Asia bears down;
you never been so put upon

your whole life and it is your life
so you are moaning *it don't mean nothin'*
and it doesn't

and that's what you keep track of
it's all you care about and that's too much
one more day, one more dark

one more dying:
so you lie awake and repeat
hometown, girlfriend

say *'59 Ford coupe*

willing to drive her everywhere
getting it on in the back seat forever.

Willing, you wanted to join
you had to go faraway
for the first time

maybe kill someone
live through it,
learn what that means.

It was a set up.
They knew this would spin your wheels.
They knew it could take years to slow down.
And they knew this could never be home anymore
never again
again.

So all you got to do is practice releasing
say to yourself a hundred times
the war is over and drift into dream.

You could wake up believing
some of those children were saved.

EVERYDAY WOOD FOR THE CROSS

Oh! We pump them up
all snaps and straps and ammo pouches
teach them steps:
new guys trying to get it right
blend into jungle
at one with thorny vines.

Dressed like snakes
brassy belts of sixty ammo
it almost looks fun
fingers triggered
like skipping school
something to write home about
something to die for

HISTORY

We don't know ourselves well
we search hard in circles
memory makes us dance
again around the fire
blood on our faces
shiny in the night

SIX KINDS OF TOUGH SHIT

The given has taken
another warrior, another kid,
doofus fuck from 3rd platoon,
whose only job was breathing

but isn't now except in gasping
gurgles from a neck wound then
moaning too much morphine and
strapped to a jungle penetrator
dangles from that chopper

lift his ass out
when the cable snaps
drops him forty fuckin' feet

through triple canopy treetops
so now, snagged twenty feet above the ground,
someone must climb for the body

ROCK 'N' ROLL WAR

What you think is a face
is a lake
is a lake
is a lake a door
an empty ladder
between memory and
a big blond kid from Kansas
shook like a leaf
'til he flopped like a fish
'til he died on the jungle floor—
each gesture stiff in phrases
like they repeat
something about survival
seems to fit around the pain
and becomes one music,
you can damn near sing along.

VOYAGE

You been nineteen too long and you know it
every day and you count them
you're tired of smelling nineteen.

You wonder about god
like he lives next door
like he cares about this shit
or is it Saturday
you can buy a ticket on a boat
but where are the postcards.

So think about Debbie in Dallas,
she drives a pickup, your pickup,
think she might be banging your best friend
write home about that?

You'd rather slide through the trees
everything you own in a pack on your back.

EVEN THE SPOON IS A WEAPON

Let's say you're chewing gum
No let's say you read a poem called gum and
English doesn't work the way you think
like it was an obstacle course
tangled in long sentences
knotted here in red
words heat up
flames appear
the story glows on…

Whatever knot the sentence
the road twists black
as an Ozarks childhood
summer's aluminum canoe
floating a clear river
as if grace were a place
a campfire on a gravel bar
a cooler full of Cokes and cookies
you reach in reading then
across the pain into the scars
triple canopy An Khe '69.
Sit ambush above a sleeping hooch
in the last gray of daylight
green turns black
two boys show up from Laos

your worst dream in 81-mm mortars
the same forever you know each night
the Battle for No Place
the pinball heart of America
200 rounds in three minutes

Memory as a swarm
smeared across the page
you carve away so much
you carry your soul
like you handle a knife
slice through fifth grade
to reach the wounded
who want to talk baseball
tell stories about the *Holley* 4-barrel
how to burn down the street
in Chevy's new three-ninety-six
As close as words get
stitched in the paddies
ankle-deep in death
which is not capitalized
and snatches things
in the name of the Nam.

THE MEAT FEES

Woven or laced over the tongue
gobs and clots strung along sung
words show how they left themselves
soldier boys face down in the muck.

I write as if you watch
the orange splash flash spread
through that green speed
over Vinh Thanh village
in that order.
You see palms that look like bent matches
burnt bent matchsticks
and running children crying
meaning passed swollen into flames.
Big chunks you don't recognize
show up red one place
you could be digging there at twilight
stuff scattered on the jungle floor
whatever facts come in
the tough kind spills
letter by letter into
nights you button down
suck it in your foxhole

BINH DINH BLUES

In this kid you are the dream
just reaching first light
you're with a learning band
that would rather play baseball
but you practice blowing
a short large-belled trumpet
shiny shiny
you cannot find the notes
blowing blown helicopter
whole thing tilting
hot approach version
you're not quite looking straight down
through no door but close enough
you do have the belt on
those boats are fishermen
bobbing in the waves off Qui Nhon
central coast of always always
all teenage death cult crap
so you have to get closer
bass line so deep
you hope it's your heart
something to do with picking a thick tree
never standing in a firefight
and steady step by step

it carries you
a no moon night
northeast of An Khe
eighteen plus N.V.A. walking the trail
ten meters from your sleeping position
and you're awake

VANISHING LESSONS

The idea was to split
and half the platoon
would crawl above the trail
while the rest slide down
climb back over the rocks
catch them in a cross fire,
kill them all
kill them all.

CURSES

When all you get is what you got
and that's given over
to staying alive on a goddamn jungle hill top
the goddamn dinks don't let go
and the goddamn rain doesn't either
and goddamn Sarge is in a goddamn bag
and goddamn evening slips into darkness
off road in the goddamn soul
you live through enough
to know who goddamn owns it.

WHERE WERE WE

Once upon a time from your left, he says,
words catch us in their doing,
move us round in the past,
dusty attic boxes.

From *the remembers*, he says.
What dreams would be
if dreams danced and
blurred to words:
the history of hurt using full sentences,
the flash and blast of last night's *delta tango*.

So he marks the breaks and pivots on the floor
tries again the moves he needs to cross the dark:
as if anywhere could be far enough
and blue did not fill his heart
with the full heat of those vast rice paddies
in Binh Dinh near Bong Son before breakfast.

CONTINGENCY

As if the way through
was a very long list,
words that work like magic
held just long enough
so poets lined them up again
as if they played redemption's song
and the way out of war
was singing that list loud
pronouncing each syllable
rolling down the page
to the door metaphor
and open it
squeaky if swung back
images stacked like freight cars
in a train wreck
like pickup sticks
reach in

SAY ALL THE WORDS

I can make the shadow dog easy,
the fish bird, and, a passable clown,
but not hold them long enough for a laugh;
then all the lights go—
and still I work that war by hand,
maybe it was a wolf.
It went in streaks
for a week, maybe ten days
a B-40 rocket breakfast call
then a few days of small arms surprises
scattered through quiet
long enough for nervous
Mercado and Hobson were always with me,
Cassidy on Compass, Flak as Mr. Delta Tango
The whole time, Big M as R.T.O. and Hobson
was Mad Dog when we needed one.
And then I went home.

At first I couldn't believe my photos
from the war. They seemed to float
in something I had lost or tossed deliberate
like a grenade into thick brush.
Nothing rhymed for me, so I put them
down a long time, maybe ten years, and
just wrote those Binh Dinh trails

to nowhere, up and down the hills,
wading rivers, outdoors monsoon fifty days
all of the above by heart—
words silhouette what we cannot keep.

WE DID OUR OWN STUNTS

Locked in love with come true
We wanted words to sing
As thick as history and
Echo in your heart.

We want them to tell you
How we are the who we were,
We hope you can remember
Darkness is older,
Night seems longer.

ECHO

We don't know ourselves well
We search hard in circles
Memory makes us dance
Again around the fire
Blood on our faces
Shiny in the night.

SOMEWHERE WITH ELVIS

Here we are, the only way we can be:
caught in these emblems and
peeking out this inky page.

He has conjured us again,
cast in words for loss.
Lamentations: chopper down,

booby-trapped multi-fragment
gunshot wounds that brought
us to bandages and turned them

red and left us dead in pieces
strewn across L.Z. Pain.
The dude, arms reaching to guide

the big bird down, to haul
our bodies out, is scared.
So we linger in these letters

keening the syllables
like the song every war makes
dopey hope and *mercymercyme*

EVERY MEAL IS A HAPPY MEAL

We don't know how far
we go on foot

and learn by smell
to talk like soldiers,

then eat the burnt offering.

VETERANS AFFAIRS

Walk into a butcher shop, draw a number.
Everybody gets two wives,
a taste of hard drugs,
some time in the slammer.
You want to add it up—
the O.D.'s, "one cars,"
guys who suck off a twelve gauge.
By the time you figure out
half your friends are dead,
you're afraid of the totals.
Waiting can take hours, then
march across to the counter
you have orders
grill burgers for supper.

You watch everything
sometimes you see faces,
you know they are children,
you know their destination.

Walk into a butcher shop

SALVAGE FOR J.O.B., JR.

Maybe that war was a '66 Chevy—
four door six banger white Nova
on blocks out back 'til '79
then tilting orange at the curb
ticketed, towed away in '82.

IT WAS A LONG TIME BEFORE THE BONES SPOKE

I can explain myself as a soldier,
lessons of blood earned by heart.
I can reach through words
and pull you closer to war,
the one you paid for,
rung by sung a saga
history misses in its rumble through the ruins.
Glimpse glitter green tracers at Fire Base Nervous,
small unit tactics with indirect fire near L.Z. Shithole,
booby traps and body bags up the Song Con,
later, in a footnote, we die there.

Oh! babies in the third-degree order of burns.
I don't remember which day on the short count,
but one clear memory dances me,
dodging bullets behind a grave mound,
Oh! blessed mothers of Agent Orange,
in a cemetery east of Pleiku.
Oh! little sister to the holy flames of Napalm:
they put their children in the ground,
wail a song that becomes my bones

THE STORY OF THE WORDS I USE

I put my bones down in the dark
night is a boat
sleep is a trip
words run together and point
like blood in the street
clot and ripple
on the rocks
catch ink and hold
a breath
an echo
the shadow of an echo
clatters past
as if Nam was a place
scraped from my brain
and splattered here explain.

REALITY TELEVISION, 1969

I thought I knew the way
through words to tell
again the soldier's take,
how language harbors
expectations—and
not just the wasteful carnage
of youthful courage cut down
for a culture that needs
their blood to purpose
what little poetry
can be made of their passing—
what marks those boys slaughtered:
they were sent like you flush the toilet
to a war no one wanted anymore,
so they gave it to the children,
let them play with death
watched them die on TV during supper.

WHAT LOVE MAKES OF US

I was somewhere again
Between history and a hard place
When my wife notices faraway

Tosses her comment ten thousand miles
Spans an ocean to reach my heart
Down there in the wind

I thought I could wait it out
Let the war go dust and blow away
Like Oklahoma in April of 1935

She could hear clouds scrape through dark

NIGHT WITHOUT HOURS

It was like all the words at once
had fled and not in sentences or
anything like a river—nothing was
alphabetized—they just lined up
and marched away from me and
I knew never coming back
as I listened to a Viet
moan to death from deep dusk
into three A.M. jungle darkness.

After the explosions and all the racket
small arms fire on rock 'n' roll
I first felt grateful to have my life
and my friends' lives in the dark
uninjured. We thought we knew
exactly how survive alive could mean.

But now, fifty years into later, when nothing
seems to matter much but money in America,
I watch morning ooze through the forest
seep over those boys blown
bloody in halves or head shot and know
exactly why we carry scary in our hearts.

TOUGH LOVE

I thought I put those boys to bed
settled in their hometown soil,
beyond the sleights and slanders
their service earned them,
but now the living cannot let them go

Over and over they try hard
to make home matter,
parades and banners
billboards and bumper stickers
"Welcome Home Heroes"
the place is sick with flags

THE UNRELIABLE INNOCENCE OF MEMORY

I want the guy
holding the photo
of a kid in jungle cammies
clutching an M-16
to look up and let go.

CLOSE ENCOUNTERS OF THE WORST KIND

I swear just as twilight tumbles purple
down the body count aisle
a three-man N.V.A. patrol

stumbles into our trip flare glare and
dashes through the center of our circle
to the dark side—

one hurdles your father's hammock—
it was his birthday, I remember—
him dropping his peaches and pound cake
but this is not his birthday poem...

this is about staying awake in the blank black
big ears in a heartbeat.

LABYRINTH

This bubbles up from somewhere
I can only reach in words
as if the past were true
and I knew the place by heart
as if our ass sad little war
is never over and
we keep giving children

MEAT FEE

That youth was taken from us, no doubt,
That our deaths were often shitty deals, is true,

And friends made monstrous mistakes in tiny *villes*, for sure;
And ones called survivors crawled away

From that great black wall of names
And their nation went in shame without them.

PEACE WITH HONOR

For so long I thought redemption lay
with Richard Milhous Nixon
shackled to a rail at the base of the Wall
and every damn daily for food he must
traverse the length of those dead boys to eat.

AIR ASSAULT

All day in the mouth of a myth
we wait for choppers
catch our lives a great lift
tilt into wind and blow
to a hilltop jungle clearing
shoot people we don't know.

DEAD SOLDIERS DAY

After the parade, after
the black wall with every body's name
after the dirt has taken them
away with the given

And you've folded the flag
it's found a drawer
and you've had supper
the late news
a bath

You lie down
want to hear a story
learn the rescue
recognize the heart beats
say the names
repeat them

MATINS

I rise from the ashes of sleep
And think I have a handle on the dark
Know the place by heart
As if night was a jungle
That had one voice
And whispers grace
Over the gristle that holds me.

THUMBNAIL

Maybe you get a bed,
maybe, they let you wear boots,
or, maybe the awful always bites your ass surprise
some silly mystic smile
as if reaching into death were real
and you squeeze some noise
some squeak and squeal—
a new contract with cold
part payment layaway
on the body waiting for you.

FEDERAL CEMETERY DIRGE

Imagine men on their knees trimming around stone

a sprinkler system at sunset
the drift of light through water

through beads of waters
like it was a book of poems
paddies squared copper
a bunch of fully-armed teenagers
the dream of dry socks
I mean really

we did not know how to act
the war we were raised for and
something going on they wouldn't tell us

Imagine all the blood it takes to keep that green
then every two weeks the mower
let's say people you know are here
Imagine the gods make up after this

CAMPAIGN RIBBONS

We are making it home
gathered still in the thickest
believing believing there was something
to die for—the minute I landed
lungs full of shit,
the tropic weight
of air, of everything
on hold: what men do
for those they kill—
we painted our faces
snuck into daylight
like living in a cloud
it was blue that gave us away
over lines down trenches
we dug for our hearts.

After we were seen
we flew the flag
against the sky—try to figure
what was lost, what is next
and where you will let that
take you, wanting it back
in one piece, when will you
let go stop asking
for another rendition.

LONG PLAYING

The past is everything it could be
The unreliable innocence of memory
Asleep in its scars
Some place to come from
In the messy order of blood
Some time making a story
In the body count of days
We tell enough to keep our secrets
History as an Ozarks playground
Mother drops a nickel in and it's all back and
Forth in a silver space coupe at Woolworth's
Or up and down on the pink pony at the grocery
Cheerios, pop beads, hula hoops
Then spinning tie-dyed lava lamps
And we gather to the herd and cheer
Our high school team at homecoming
Grinning grainy in the snapshots
In the patchwork light of language
Doo-wop duck and cover, frisbees
Memory as a large glass bowl of matchbooks
That stretch of county gravel going home
Live fire low crawl monkey tricks in the jungle
Some far-off country heart of the country
A place worn smooth
Holds us warm like a whisper

LIQUIDS

Jungle wise who knows
what grows there deep?
More stream than consciousness,
each word rivers its own banks.

Language holds us everywhere we have said.
Most like weeds,
we root in our tears,

trying to hold loss,
talking shiny to the blind.
Lying in piss warm paddy water

You learn what metaphors kill,
machine guns punctuate, and,
guys die for what they cannot pronounce.

They carried love in their hearts
like water to a fire
in a sleeping child's room.

"VIETNIZATION"

You're in this someplace else you dream.

Night a thing, tough shit all over darkness
you talk with the medic who picks up the pieces

He tells you he's tired of the hours
long hours bending, the explosions,
weird Viet songs up through the brush
one damn thing for sure he says
next time I won't run short of bags
these guys get greased

they're going out like they're supposed to
no more makeshift crap

Some asshole back home can afford it

HOUSTON SPRING, 2010

In the fairy tale that sets you free
It's pickup truck month in Texas
April pushes pink tea roses through chain link
Pecans flash out life green
Purple irises surround the patio
And the black smoker/broiler sets there cold
So it is difficult to see our Afghan war
Clotted in the shadows near the white picnic table

PART TWO

What truth is it
that makes men so miserable?

—Robert Creeley

THE OTHER HALF OF EVERYTHING

It may be I don't remember enough to tell the story.

It may be I don't remember.

I might have to rebuild portions. Refurbish
memory. What I do get back can seed the rest.

I could have it all.

If not the first go, then the second, third.

Every minute I spend thinking *from now on*
this changes otherwise, is permanent.

Extrapolations shorthand, so to speak.

Each night they all want to talk desire.
As if it had to do with survival.

Sheer love. Listen

If I could do this, say it, a prayer for the
destruction of helicopters, first there would
be one for Politicians.

Capital p.

All of them.

You almost have to lie. By now we got so much shit
on this we don't hear otherwise. Lies. Free float-
ing terror. Vietnam vets. Free fire zones. You
heard it all. You know the tune.

I, for one, am dropping constraints. I'll hold it
to language. More mischief, less mystery.

Just words. A split infinitive.

You don't have to take it on the chin.
Leave the darkness to Springsteen.
I know the tune.
Any time now is fifty years since.

Not always New Year's Day. Not January First.
Beyond counting. One at a time. Down. Per
day, a year older. Per annum yield.

It does take great clots of peanut butter.
And where does music fit?
Between hand grenades and H-bombs?
In the past perfect?

Duct tape, vise grips, WD-40.

What distance the need?

Ben cranks the right nut off the bike's rear wheel.
Dug in, slightly, he opens the gears, lifts the...
You can still call it a bike. You couldn't ride it.
He is thinking about the war but his hands are busy.
He holds on. It's cool. He unscrews the valve. De
flates, hums. 1969. Pleiku Province. 4th Combat
Engineers. Sixth bridge out QL 19. This is
the third time he has helped replace it and the N.L.F.
isn't waiting for them to finish. This is first person.
The first, at least, he killed with a shovel.

Outside the wire, melody doesn't work.

You're waiting for something to happen.

It's your life. You forget you are waiting.
You forget what law this makes.

Whose song which night?
Vietnam taught me to survive mistakes. Even
ones planned carefully over thirty years. Ones
that kill several million people. But not me.
Not you.

I was a kid. O.K.?
You have the ultimate faith, things work out.
Hula hoops and frisbees

I think the soul is more like gristle.
He still doesn't know how he did it. Then he
does. Spinning, tight, he pulls the tire from
the rim. Sets them both down.

I lost a year that way. Fifty-two weekends.

Whatever they use for memory here doesn't work.
I am talking details—time of the crime crap—
"circles and arrows, eight by ten..."

You want me to ease off. That's the problem.
Everybody eased off some. The fate of baseball.
It is better on TV.

We are 100% alert. Everything by ear.

I learned one thing in the jungle. You can
learn it from a book. You recognize the writ-
ing. Perfect helicopter in there. Perfect
text.

Everybody see the words?

The first page is always a map, you see
where you are from the start.

Follow the bouncing Betty.

Somewhere in the 60's Sgt. Friday saying,
"Just the facts, ma'am, just the…"

Then the fucking duck comes down with money.

They told us not to keep letters from home.
In case you get zapped. V.C. take them, the letters,
send them to the peaceniks and they
harass your parents.

Imagine all the red it takes to make this true.
Flash forward.

You're an expert on dreaming.
I need a few minutes to get through the overture.
Every fifth round is a tracer.
Ready for explosions?

And over and over the little neon "fuck
you" sign keeps going off.

All I wanted was center field, the grass cut...

I wish they would harass my folks.

You got the words and in the back of your mind
you could win a million dollars. Someone named
Ed is shaking your hand... yearly payments for
how long?

That takes a few minutes also.

Not walking but double time.

It has to do with the year of your birth.

You could get away believing
salvation includes a car. The car.

Where's the moon on this? The stars?

Nobody loses sleep over Nam anymore? Did
they? Did you? No one refers to Nam as a
theater of war like they did for the Second.

"Chinese Border War"

Act II, scene i: Tropical version.

You think there is more so you want some.

Pop beads, hula hoops, Cheerios.

Hey, cube the totals.

"These are events which alter and illuminate
our time and you are...ready?"

It could involve you. Twenty-five words or less.

Serpents, imagination. You know. Here
in the hopelessly overstated, in the midst
of a poem...
It becomes a level of testosterone.

Silastic penile implants.

Three hundred sixty-five dailies.
If you can get closer you see the dead.

You remember the war.

Dimmer switch, clutch plate, power train.

Scores at eleven.

Already I am making up excuses. There are
plenty of excuses. You learn one thing—
excuses don't cover your ass. Might help
you sleep. Dreamland. If that is where you
are going. Disney World.

That might help. Think Vietnam was a theme park
for working class kids.
Let's drink some beer. Get it?

You want an answer? Here's one! Here's the
answer—this is the final surge of something
Hittites started. You can call it progress.
Sometimes it is.

Smell them.

Twenty years from now I will not keep track
of the war. That's what it taught. Not to…
Keep it spinning.
It's over in no time.
Cognate, there.

Which poem is it now?

It could be the garden of the Emperor.
the fade on the wall, grass moist green,
full of water and someone named Ed...
This is where the tubas kick in
and I don't want to miss a note.

Frame edges border square.

You're already in the league.
So what's another night rolling the ball?

If I want to go on forever, I'll have to
hold a Schlitz to get there.

Some things are facts and some things are you.

Me.

And a T-shirt to make it valid.

Eternal Automotive. Perpetual Bearings.
I heard today "ring around the rosy" is a
song from the days of the Black Death.

14th century.

You get a year to die,
you count the days.

You learn to call anything survival.

It can be big enough to hold childhood.

Will someone hit sustain?
Fast forward?

I am waiting 'til my body calls out for coffee.

There is almost not an interval.

We were talking desire.

A few of the guys aren't here tonight. Scott,
Officer Puke from the Big Red One. He got
a story I don't recognize. He is full of that
story. He wants to adjust. He can make it
in a culture that has to be able to destroy
the world in order to survive. He wants to come
home to a country that's ready to do it again

Act III.

All you need is a little AK fire and
you can kill everyone in here.

If I could get the numbers right
I would count them.

I can rhyme "pocket full of posy"
but I won't give away the deal with the wire.

Insider references you can't handle. French
phrases. And the argument is going elsewhere.

Spacing large distances immense.

Nobody in this room this evening
will mention suicide, so I have to say it.
The rate is rather alarming. It's not like
the selective service.

Did everyone get a number?

Wonder what that does to memory?

Not so much that my memories are pleasant.
But as a statement to my survival.

I do want to get that right.

Trochaic.

Or this could be about football only
we don't get paid much.
You think there is more...
Someone in the jungle yelling in Vietnamese.
I don't say anything about it but I can al-
most figure what they are saying. Not what
they are saying but what it means.

Like the movie but no music and it stinks.
I lost my place.
You know, screw anything thirty years there's
bound to be withdrawal.

I was young and I remember.

I thought I could fill enough sandbags.

Leave the tropics and go straight home.

Expect to live at peace in the heart of a
military empire. Every day martial pumped
at you. White lines in your blue sky.

Newspaper versions.
That pile of books about Nam.

One end of the wire woven in your crotch.

You wonder if camouflage works.

Remember.

Doo-wop duck and cover.

Ashes, ashes.

You get an E for attendance.

All of the above.

You become fucked. You are glad you made it.

NOTES

A claymore is a command-detonated anti-personnel mine.

An Khe is a town in Binh Dinh Province.

Vinh Thanh is a village on the Song Con in Binh Dinh Province.

Binh Dinh is a coastal province in central Vietnam.

N.V.A. is the People's Army of Vietnam.

Bong Son is a town situated on a vast rice paddy plain in Binh Dinh.

"Say All the Words" is for Gary Cassidy, the late John Hobson, and Ray "Tuco" Mercado.

"Reality Television, 1969" is for my daughter Rachel.

Cammies is an informal term for camouflage clothing.

M-16 is the U.S.-issued automatic assault rifle, a standard weapon used by American troops in Vietnam.

"Close Encounters of the Worst Kind" is for Joe P. "Flak" Hannigan.

"Liquids" is a memorial for Dennis Dotson, Robert Goselin, Robert Hill, and Steven Stefanski; all four were killed in action June 5, 1970. Helicopter shot down.

The N.L.F. refers to the National Liberation Front, or as called by U.S. troops, the Viet Cong.

"The Other Half of Everything" is for Ron Gleason.

ACKNOWLEDGEMENTS

The following poems originally appeared, some in different forms, in *The Iowa Review*, where they received second place in the 2016 Jeff Sharlet Memorial Award for Veteran Writing, judged by Phil Klay: "Ghost of a Person Passing in Front of the Flag," "Rock 'n' Roll War" (as "Happy Valley above Vinh Thanh,") "Fractured Fairy Tale," "Six Kinds of Tough Shit," "It Was a Long Time Before the Bones Spoke," "The Story of the Words I Use," and "Reality Television, 1969."

These poems appeared, in slightly different versions, in the following journals: "The Other Half of Everything," *Ironwood*, the final issue, 1989; *Assuming Blue* in *War, Literature & the Arts*, 2005; and *Even the Spoon Is a Weapon* as a chapbook from Inleaf Press, 2005.

Individual poems have appeared in: *The Iowa Review, Colorado Review, Five Fingers Review, Transfer, Barque, North American Review, San Pedro River Review, War, Literature & the Arts*, and *Veterans for Peace Newsletter*; and/or anthologized in *Practicing Angels, Inheritance of Light, American War Poetry, Carrying the Darkness, Unwinding the Vietnam War*, and *Unaccustomed Mercy*.

The author is grateful for the camaraderie of Bernard Gershenson, Ron Gleason, Paula Gocker, Howard Hilliard, Matthew Martinez, Jr., and Randy Twaddle and knows he would not have come so far without them. Mark Dostert gets a double down *muchas gracias* for his encouragement and faith in these poems.

Same goes for the Bravo Boys of the First of the Fourteenth Infantry (The Right of the Line), 1969–70. There is no now for me that is not soaked in their bravery and sacrifice.

Thanks also to Jessica Cole, Phuc Luu, and Kate Martin Williams of Bloomsday for making a beautiful home for the poems.

Added thanks to Howard Hilliard for the title, on loan from one of his beautiful pinhole camera images, and Randy Twaddle for the cover art, "Birds and Bombs," charcoal on paper, 22x30, 1989.

P. 6.   John Wayne

CPSIA information can be obtained
at www.ICGtesting.com
Printed in the USA
FFOW03n2053130418
46232890-47589FF

9 780999 823910